The New Restorationists

A Critique of Frank Viola and George Barna's "Pagan Christianity?"

Albert M. McIlhenny

The New Restorationists: A Critique of Frank Viola and George Barna's "Pagan Christianity?"

Copyright © 2010

ISBN 978-0-557-46221-6

Albert M. McIlhenny

All Rights Reserved

Table of Contents

Introduction   5

Chapter 1 – Basic Misconceptions
    1.1 – Postmodern Restorationism   7
    1.2 – Decontextualization   9
    1.3 – Conclusion   11

Chapter 2 – Church Buildings
    2.1 – Church and "Church"   13
    2.2 – Domus Ecclesiae   14
    2.3 – Constantine   18
    2.4 – Constantine's Basilicas   20
    2.5 – Gothic Cathedrals   27
    2.6 – Protestant Church Buildings   30
    2.7 – Conclusion   31

Chapter 3 – Church and Liturgy
    3.1 – Origins of the Liturgy   33
    3.2 – Sermons   35
    3.3 – Conclusion   37

Chapter 4 – Church Authority
    4.1 – Hierarchy in the New Testament   39
    4.2 – Pastoral Offices   42
    4.3 – Conclusion   45

Chapter 5 – Sacraments of the Church
    5.1 – Baptism   47

5.2 – Lord's Supper	48
5.3 – Conclusion	51

Chapter 6 – Miscellaneous Issues

6.1 – Christian Education	53
6.2 – Using the Bible	54
6.2 – Conclusion	55

Chapter 7 – Final Conclusions 57

Appendix – Book Review 59

Introduction

Pagan Christianity? It is an eye-catching title that appeals to the sensationalism in all of us. A title with a question that asks if the faith of the Church is really pagan and answers emphatically yes. This time, however, it comes not from an opponent of the Christian faith as with *Zeitgeist* but from fellow Christians. Nor are they alone – many fundamentalist websites across the internet preach the same message and these often go back to such "classics" as Alexander Hislop's *Two Babylons*. Yes, folks, Christianity is all pagan but you can get back to the real Jesus if you follow [fill in the name of the particular restorationist movement or pseudo-Christian cult]. It's that simple.

This will be an examination of the views presented by Frank Viola and George Barna in their work. Viola has been a leader in the "house church" movement for some time. Barna is a well known Christian pollster. Their book is a revision of Viola's earlier *Pagan Christianity: The Origin of Our Modern Church Practices*. The question we must ask is this: Do they have a case for their views?

I believe the answer is an emphatic no. There are so many basic errors and abuses of citations that the book is rendered completely unreliable. Every now and then they may actually have a good point but it is lost amidst the rubble of distortions, falsehoods, and double standards. There may yet be a good book making the case for house churches – this one is not that book.

However, we live in a time when conspiracy sells and sensationalism is king. The over the top accusations have hit a nerve and an answer needs to be provided. Many Christians have already done so but were reluctant to raise some issues because it might seem to accuse the pair of

6   *The New Restorationists*

dishonesty. I will not make any judgment on that but I will raise some of these issues here and let the chips fall where they may. It may be they were relying on secondary sources misquoting these authors or they are just not very good researchers. But it is quite obvious that, at the very least, they have not done their homework.

I make no judgment on the idea of house churches and certainly do not wish to label them all as followers of Viola and Barna. But they do exert some influence in those circles and it is time someone called them on their misrepresentations of evidence.

I suggest you have their book in hand as well as a Bible. Examine the evidence and ask yourself this question: Have they been honest with the evidence?

Chapter 1 – Basic Misconceptions

Frank Viola has recently risen to become a leading critic of how the Church operates. There are two things that set Viola apart, however, from other critics of the Church. The first is that Viola is a Christian. The second is that he is not criticizing the way the Church operates now but how it has operated for close to two thousand years. From Viola's standpoint, the Church went off the narrow road shortly after the last Apostle died and its been all downhill since.

1.1 – Postmodern Restorationism

Viola is not just someone who is spitting in the wind. He has gained a loyal following and is recognized as a major figure within the "house church" movement. While not every house church participant embraces his views , he does speak for a significant percentage of those within this growing movement.

In a series of books giving his vision of church history and true Christianity, Viola has engaged in a large degree of historical revisionism by recasting many church practices as inherently pagan and promoting his vision of the teaching of Jesus and the Apostles. His vision shares common ground with various restorationist works of the past century[1] – a

---

1 These include, but are not necessarily limited to such books as *Two Babylons* by Alexander Hislop, *Trail of Blood* by J. M. Carroll, *The Pilgrim Church* by E. H. Broadbent, *The History of the New Testament Church* by Peter S. Ruckman, and *Roman Catholicism* by Lorraine Boettner. Three of them (Hislop, Broadbent, and

8   The New Restorationists

vision that has garnered wide appeal for those who wish Christianity were less historical and more American.

This book will concentrate on examining the claims of the most well known of Viola's books: *Pagan Christianity?: Exploring the Roots of Our Church Practices*. This book, recently revised in a second edition with Christian pollster George Barna, gives Viola's most detailed views on Christian history. With Barna's name added to the mix, even more attention has been given to his ideas and it is becoming cited regularly in "free church" circles.

That Viola and Barna makes the claims they do is not necessarily a shock. As mentioned, others have done so in the past. What is interesting are the extensive footnotes that give the appearance of research to back up their claims. But have they really? I have seen a number of church historians criticize the book but none have taken the time to examine many of the referenced sources. If they had, they might be in for a surprise. It turns out their extensive citations are far less than meets the eye.

Viola's version of the "house church" movement is the latest installment of that great American pastime known as "Christian restorationism" whereby modern – or in this case postmodern – American Christians decide the Church as passed down in history is apostate and they will restore it. One immediately wonders about their presumption to restore what they believe God has failed to maintain for close to two millennia. Such attempts at "restoring" the Church inevitably end up looking more like something those of their era would come up with than something that would exist in the first century A.D. That is, their "restored church" looks more like themselves than the Apostles.

This is in stark contrast to the idea of Reformation that seeks to remove those elements contrary to the Biblical faith. Reformers do not expect to go back to some idealized church of the first century they create in their imaginations. They accept the Church will evolve over time but insist it

---

Boettner) are cited by Viola & Barna in *Pagan Christianity?*

Chapter 1 – Basic Misconceptions

maintain the faith once delivered to the saints.

This is not a book I relish writing. With so many attacks upon the faith from those outside the Church, the last thing we need is to have Christians going at each other. However, the charges Viola has made are a complete misrepresentation of Christian history and casts derision upon those of past centuries who often paid the ultimate price for being a follower of Christ. This is not to say any era of the Church's history is perfect and the times Violas describes are very much a mixed bag. But his presentation exaggerates the negatives and never even raises the issue of the many positive things that happened during those centuries. If one is to criticize, the criticism should be honest. On this point, Viola and Barna have let the church down.

1.2 – Decontextualization

The approach taken by Frank Viola and George Barna is apparent almost from the first page. They dislike how the Church has operated for the last few millennia and they are out to change it. Moreover, they are quite sure God sees it the same way. The never address why God has been putting up with it for close to two thousand years or why it took the Holy Spirit so long to leading us to all truth as promised. But it doesn't matter because there is a new sheriff in town.

Viola and Barna begin their analysis by employing a technique almost identical to that of skeptics in the Jesus Seminar: they decontextualize the message of Jesus and the Apostles. They assume the early Church broke from the practices of Judaism and those of the later Church were largely pagan in origin. Hence, like skeptics, they presume a movement that bore no influence of the Judaism from which it arose and passed on no influence to the Church that followed.

The absurdity of this position should not need to be pointed out. The Apostles were observant Jews who understood Jesus in the context of Second Temple Judaism. But this will not do for Viola and Barna since

10   The New Restorationists

they cannot have a Jewish Christianity. After all, the Jews worshipped in buildings reserved for that specific use under a hierarchical structure with rabbis and elders leading the people in their order of worship. If the early Christians were maintaining connections with Judaism, then the practices they criticize might well have been Jewish rather than pagan in origin.

The disconnection from Judaism is essential for Viola and Barna's thesis. Any link between the early Church and Judaism undermines their claims of succumbing to paganism. For their argument to have any force, the break must be sudden and complete. However, even a cursory reading of the New Testament demonstrates such a thesis to be patently false.[2]

No less problematic is their view the early Church was a non-hierarchical, non-ritualistic, non-liturgical organism.[3] Any claims there was no hierarchy needs to explain why one of the Church's first actions was to select a replacement for Judas and give qualifications for the office.[4] Moreover, throughout the New Testament we see leadership being exercised by the Apostles.[5] Paul appeals to the confirmation of his message by the Church's leadership[6] and his own status as an Apostle as evidence of his authority.[7] Paul also points out the importance of the Church offices of presbyter and deacon and gives qualifications to hold

---

2   See *Acts* 10:9-16. Peter's comments show that even at this late point he is still an observant Jew and this is the norm among Christians. Even by Acts 15, the admission of gentiles without conversion to Judaism opens a major rift in the Church and the practice is clearly a novelty for the Church.
3   *Pagan Christianity?*, 27.
4   *Acts* 1:20-26
5   For example, the early Church is said to have devoted themselves to the Apostles' teaching (*Acts* 2:42); the Apostles had the authority to introduce a new position within the Church by appointing seven to delegate duties (*Acts* 6:1-6); although Philip could baptize, the Apostles were required for the laying on of hands (*Acts* 8:14-17); the Apostles and elders meet in council at Jerusalem and decide the fate of the Gentile mission (*Acts* 15). Those denying the Apostles were the leaders of the Church and were recognized as such is simply ignoring the text of Scripture itself in favor of their own presuppositions.
6   *Galatians* 2:1-2; *Acts* 15.
7   *I Corinthians* 15:5-11

Chapter 1 – Basic Misconceptions

these titles.[8]

The absurdity of denying rituals ignores the obvious links of baptism to the Jewish mikvah, the form of the Eucharist with its words of institution[9], the numerous references to the laying on of hands[10], and the instructions for the anointing of the sick.[11] It is rather difficult to maintain a non-ritualist view of the early Church. The implication the authors wish to make is that "ritual" equals "pagan" but any reading of the Old Testament will demonstrate that the Jews were commanded to fulfill rituals by God. Ritual implies liturgy and a liturgical context is assumed in references to the prayers, the Lord's Supper, the breaking of bread, and praying on certain hours.[12] It is clear the early Church followed Jewish praxis under the leadership of the Apostles in the early decades of the Church.

1.3 – Conclusion

Viola and Barna's analysis of the Church throughout history begins with a misstep that affects everything subsequently discussed. The slant and misdirection are obvious from the very first page. At no point do they ever try to approach the evidence from anything other than their own biases even when the overwhelming consensus of their own sources states otherwise. Their slant, perhaps more subtle in the first few chapters, descends into an unfair attack upon the memory of Christians of past centuries without any attempt to understand the specific context of their

---

8 *I Timothy* 3:1-13; *Titus* 1:5-9
9 *I Corinthians* 11:23-26
10 *Acts* 6:6; *Acts* 8:17-18; *Acts* 8:18; *Acts* 9:12; *Acts* 9:17; *Acts* 13:3; *Acts* 19:6; *Acts* 28:8; *I Timothy* 4:14; *I Timothy* 5:22; *2 Timothy* 1:6; *Hebrews* 6:2
11 James 5:14-15
12 It is sometimes argued the New Testament does not give specific liturgical norms as does the Torah. However, it was written decades after the Church began and the Jewish context of the early life of the Church is self-evident and liturgy is part of that context. Examples of this are their devotion to "the breaking of bread and the prayers" and references to prayers at prescribed times that were norms for a devout Jew (Acts 10:9).

12   *The New Restorationists*

times or how they perceived the issue. Everything is judged by the standards of a rather parochial form of American Fundamentalism that has little in common with either the Church of the Apostles or the Church of history.

Chapter 2 – Church Buildings

Perhaps the most memorable part of *Pagan Christianity?* for many readers is the authors' discussion of church buildings in the patristic era and later. The places where most Christians worship each Sunday are not only presented as violations of Biblical standards but as downright pagan. Viola and Barna's approach is more often than not to throw every possible accusation at those who built them and to present the period as one of decline and compromise for the Christian faith.

I will present various claims they make against Church buildings in different eras and demonstrate how they completely misrepresent the evidence before them. I do not claim buildings of the eras discussed or any era are beyond criticism. The point is that the evidence needs to be presented fairly and at this they have failed miserably.

2.1 – Church and "Church"

When discussing Church architecture, Viola and Barna quickly turn to the use of the word "church" to denote a building. Noting the New Testament references to the Greek "ekklesia" always refers to the people of God, they consider the difference to be a cause of confusion.[13] They ignore the earliest Christians often met at the Temple in Jerusalem as well as in houses and even in rented halls. It is only after the Church separates from Judaism and grows sufficiently as a movement to warrant its own

---

13 *Pagan Christianity?*, 11-12.

buildings that this would become an issue. Even then, the Church's outlaw status prevented it from owning anything legally as an institution.

The supposed "confusion" over the term "church" for a building occurs only in the minds of the authors. It is not uncommon to use the same word to describe related aspects of the same thing. Saying you are "going to church" will no more confuse the people of God with a building than saying you are "going to the movies" will confuse the film viewed with the building where it is shown.

Nor are the authors much better when reasoning about the buildings God's people had constructed prior to the Church coming into existence at Pentecost. They claim Jesus had a negative view of the Jewish temple[14] by citing his prediction of its destruction.[15] This is a complete misrepresentation of the events. God had commanded the building of both Jewish temples[16] and Jesus had referred to the Second Temple as his Father's house.[17] The destruction of both temples was not a judgment on the buildings but on the lack of faithfulness among the people.

Even at this basic level of interpreting well known passages of Scripture, the claims of Viola and Barna are severely biased and perhaps less than honest. If they can be this careless with the Biblical record, how trustworthy can they be with the data of history? We will now begin examining that issue.

2.2 – Domus Ecclesiae

Central to Viola and Barna's claims about church buildings are the accounts of the early Church in the Book of Acts meeting in each others' homes.[18] They use this to make a connection to the domus eccleisae

---

14 *ibid*, 13.
15 *Mark* 14:58
16 *I Chronicles* 22:9-10; *Ezra* 1:1-3
17 *Luke* 2:49; *John* 2:16
18 *Acts* 2:46

Chapter 2 – Church Buildings 15

(home churches) of the patristic era and conclude the practice of meeting in each others' homes is the standard model for the Church. Thus other possible models would represent a retreat from the Biblical norms.

Anyone familiar with the New Testament, church history, or archeology would find severe problems with these claims. Moreover, the evidence provided actually fails to support their position. Take for example the early Church in Jerusalem. While it is true they met in each others' homes, they also met at the Temple.[19] Christians meet in each others' homes today for fellowship but that does not mean they do not gather on Sunday as a community in a larger building. The two concepts were not mutually exclusive then or now. Paul even used a lecture hall (presumably rented) to teach.[20] Was he unaware he should have been meeting in their homes?

The fact is the New Testament gives no indication that meeting in homes is a norm for Christian worship. Obviously a small band of followers in the early period would have gathered among themselves in homes but they continued to observe the Jewish practices at the Temple. The failure to recognize the Church arose out of Second Temple Judaism condemns Viola and Barna to repeated misunderstandings of the evidence before them.

As the Church grew, it also faced persecution from the Roman state and so continued meetings in homes was a necessity. However, as the Church grew, larger homes were donated by wealthy Christians for their use and these were actually the first "church buildings" intended as places for the community to gather as a group. Viola and Barna fail to see the distinction between such an arrangement and informal gatherings in homes and equate the domus ecclesiae with contemporary house churches in their movement. Nothing could be further from the case as the domus ecclesiae were large structures remodeled for worship that sometimes included such items as altar spaces and a baptistry.

Viola and Barna's citations for their interpretation of the domus

---

19 *Acts* 2:46; *Acts* 3.1
20 *Acts* 19:9

16   *The New Restorationists*

ecclesiae also leave something to be desired. For example, they cite Frank Senn to support their position that the Christians were just meeting in simple homes.[21] However, in the passage cited, Senn quite explicitly states the Church of this period "usually met in private residences *that had been converted* into suitable gathering spaces for the Christian community"[22] (italics mine). Thus these were residences that had been converted for use as places of worship and were not homes except for perhaps the clergy.

Viola and Barna also fail to mention how, in contrast to their beliefs, Senn explores the deep connections between church and synagogue and the liturgical nature of its worship. The entire chapter where the quoted citation appears explains how the Church's liturgy developed from Jewish practices[23] and hence Viola and Barna have completely misread the context of their source.

Astonishingly, the authors then try to use the nonexistence of church buildings other than the domus ecclesiae as further evidence church buildings were frowned upon by the early Christians. They claim the Christians could have erected church buildings if they wished and cite the seizing of their properties – many of which were quite expansive – for evidence.[24] At this point one can see how their biases affect their judgment: the seizure of property is the obvious reason why Christians did not erect other sorts of structures that would draw Rome's attention and chose to convert homes that would blend into their surroundings.

Further errors are made as they describe the excavation of a home church at Dura Europos. Viola and Barna describe the find merely as a house with a wall torn out.[25] Nowhere do they mention the walls were covered in iconography or there was a room converted into a baptistry

---

21 *Pagan Christianity?*, 14 n22.
22 Frank Senn, *Christian Liturgy: Catholic and Evangelical* (Fortress Press, 1997), 53.
23 *ibid*, 53-108.
24 *Pagan Christianity?*, 15 n23.
25 *Pagan Christianity?*, 15

Chapter 2 – Church Buildings   17

with a pool[26] or the Christian liturgical texts written in Hebrew and based upon the *Didache*.[27] A more recent find in Meggido[28] from roughly the same period only reinforces the notion these were not simple homes – and yet all of this has escaped the attention of the authors.

Also ignored is the textual evidence that refutes their claims. For example, the *Chronicles of Edessa*, a history of the ancient city, describes a flood occurring in the year 201 A.D. and details the devastation. One of the buildings destroyed was "the sanctuary of the Christians." It is hard to imagine that title being given to anything other than a building known as the Christians' regular place of worship.

As the third century wore on, there was a period of relative toleration of Christianity. Persecution was intermittent and, in some places, nonexistent. Christians were in a position to worship more openly and their home churches became far more elaborate. Some pagans such as the philosopher Porphyry criticized the ostentatious nature of these worship spaces. In a further mistake, Viola and Barna attribute Porphyry's criticism to the churches built by Constantine despite the philosopher having been quite dead years before construction began on any of the emperor's Churches.[29]

The reason for Viola and Barna's insistence the Christians worshipped in homes is to identify the current house church movement with the early Church so they may identify "worship building" with "pagan building." Both assertions are erroneous. The Jewish temple was similar in structure to many pagan temples with an inner sanctuary for the priests and outer

---

26 F. L. Cross and E. A. Livingstone, *The Oxford Dictionary of the Christian Church* (Oxford University Press, 1997), 517.
27 J. L. Teicher, "Ancient Eucharistic Prayers in Hebrew (Dura-Europos Parchment D. Pg. 25)", The Jewish Quarterly Review New Series 54.2 (October 1963), 99-109.
28 Tidhar Ofek, "Ancient Church Uncovered at Megiddo," *The Jerusalem Post*, November 8, 2005.
29 Constantine came to power in the West in 312 A.D. and the whole empire a decade later. It was then that the church building program began. Porphyry died in 305 A.D. This issue will be discussed further in section 2.4.

18   The New Restorationists

courts for various ranks of worshippers. But the "converted house" idea is also not without issues. Many homes of pagans had household shrines likely used for Christian worship upon conversion. Moreover, pagans also converted houses for worship and this was common for some mystery religions. For example, the Christians were not the only ones at Dura Europos to use a converted house – there was also a Mithraeum with a similar design. This is never discussed by Viola and Barna and the double standards become more and more obvious.

Any identification of the current house church movement with the worship of the domus ecclesiae falls apart upon closer inspection. The descriptions of worship in this period in the *Didache* and early Church Fathers such as Justin Martyr and Hippolytus was liturgical and the local church was governed by bishops and presbyters. Viola and Barna have merely projected their own modern American egalitarian sensibilities upon those from late antiquity – a questionable practice to say the least.

2.3 – Constantine

When Frank Viola and George Barna turn to the topic of the Emperor Constantine, the gloves most definitely come off. The authors show little in the way of fairness and perspective and anything bad they can find about him is aired regardless of its likely truth. As far as they are concerned, Constantine is a bad guy and whatever bad things have been said about him should be taken at face value.

This is not to defend him as a blameless saint. Someone does not get to be Roman Emperor over stiff opposition through meekness. Nor does history give rulers the title "great" because they hesitated to smash their enemies. However, he was a very complex man and the cartoonish villain the authors describe simply does not fit the historical record. When you describe someone in such terms and declare him as intentionally destructive of the Christian faith as the authors do here, you should be able to come up with something more substantial than the innuendo and

Chapter 2 – Church Buildings   19

armchair psychology on display in their exposition.

Even more shocking are the obvious distortions of the historical record and their claims to be backed up by scholars. Take for example the declaration of Sunday as a day of rest. The Christians had been worshipping on that day for centuries and Constantine declared it a day of rest when he begins showing them favor. The connection is obvious but instead Viola and Barna decide he did it because he wanted to give homage to Mithras the Unconquered Sun![30]

It gets even more surreal when one checks out their source for this strange claim: Justo Gonzalez's *The Story of Christianity*. This is a solid church history and it would be surprising if Gonzalez made such a claim – but he did no such thing. While Gonzalez mentioned the declaration, he never mentioned any such motivation.

Gonzalez mentions Constantine's prior devotion to Sol Invictus, theorized he may have thought the Unconquered Sun and the Christian God were two ways of expressing the Supreme God, and concluded Constantine's knowledge of Christianity at this stage left much to be desired.[31] In Constantine's view, Christ was the God who gave him military victories and he wished to keep his favor.[32] As for the edict on Sunday, Gonzalez describes it as intentionally worded in a neutral fashion so to gain the widest appeal.[33] While he mentions Mithraism, a popular cult among the soldiers, also had attachments to Sunday, he nowhere states that Constantine did so to honor Mithras.

A further example of Viola and Barna pinning anything on Constantine is their citing excavations around St. Peter's that turned up a mosaic with Christ in the motif of the Unconquered Sun. The authors claim this further

---

30 *Pagan Christianity?*, 19.
31 Justo L. Gonzalez, *The Story of Christianity: The Early Church to the Dawn of the Reformation* (Harper Collins, 1984), 122-123.
32 *ibid.*
33 *ibid.*

proves Constantine's affinity for sun worship[34] but this mosaic is from decades prior to Constantine coming to power! Viola and Barna's source is an article in *Christian History* magazine. There are a number of dubious assertions in that article but this one is not among them. It does mention the mosaic and states it was from "around the same time" as Constantine but the author never stated the emperor had anything to do with the mosaic.[35] Even this weaker assertion is mistaken and in a later book on the early Church the author correctly dates it to the third century.[36]

And so they go on for page after page taking every opportunity to present Constantine as something just short of the antichrist. Nowhere do they mention, for example, the Council of Nicea, the return of seized property to Christians, and other positives that occurred during the period. Nothing outside their preconceived notions ever stands a chance of mention.

2.4 – Constantine's Basilicas

Given Viola and Barna's views of Constantine the person, it should not be surprising that their views are no different for the buildings he constructed for the Church. It is also not surprising the presentation is every bit as biased and factually inaccurate as what went before.

The authors engage in an unrelenting effort to "prove" the basilicas built by Constantine were based upon pagan temple structures. This is faced with a very monumental problem: they actually were quite different from most pagan temples. The latter were usually reserved for the priests with the worship taking place outdoors in courtyards similar to the worship at the Temple in Jerusalem. The basilica design, the style of Roman civic buildings, was necessitated because Christian worship was

---

34 *Pagan Christianity?*, 19.
35 E. Glenn Hinson. "Worshiping Like Pagans?", *Christian* History, Issue 37 (1993).
36 E. Glenn Hinson, *The Early Church* (Abington, 1996), 244.

indoors in a gathering place.

It is indeed indicative of the direction the discussion is headed that they begin with one of their more memorable errors. In commenting on the grandeur of Constantine's new basilicas, Viola and Barna claim pagans asserted these edifices imitated the structure of pagan temples.[37] The evidence provided is a quote from the philosopher Porphyry chastising Christians for criticizing pagan worship while having their own grand buildings.[38]

As I mentioned earlier in section 2.2, Porphyry was quite dead by the time Constantine laid ground for any of the buildings in question. In fact, their own source clearly places Porphyry's comments sometime around 262-263 A.D.[39] – about a half century prior to Constantine's rise to power. So where do they get the idea Porphyry was writing about Constantine's basilicas? I suppose they simply assumed any negative comment about a church being elaborate in that era must have been aimed at those of Constantine because their incorrect presuppositions demand earlier churches be simple homes.

The easiest way to see their error is to examine Porphyry's comments in detail. The claim under discussion comes from his work *Against the Christians* written about 260-265 A.D. It is only available now in fragments quoted by Christian apologists in their responses and one of the fragments contains this barb aimed at the Church:

> Moreover, the Christians also, imitating the erection of the temples, build very large houses, into which they go together and pray, although there is nothing to prevent them from doing this in their own houses, since the Lord certainly hears from every place.

Not only does this appear long before any of Constantine's buildings, but

---

37 *Pagan Christianity?*, 22.
38 *ibid*, 22n80.
39 L. Michael White, *Building God's House in the Roman World* (John Hopkins, 1990), 129.

22   The New Restorationists

Porphyry clearly identifies them as *houses* built for the purpose of worship.

Note that Porphyry states the Christians *build houses they go in together and pray* – thus these are new structures and not existing homes. He also states that they could just as well pray *in their own houses* – thus indicating these are NOT their homes and are dedicated for Christian worship. These points underscore the fact that the domus eccleisae were houses converted for worship – a common practice for fledgling religious groups at the time – and not the informal house gatherings he has presupposed. Hence, far from condemning Constantine, the quote actually critiques the "house churches" Viola and Barna have made an idol and presents them as something very different than their erroneous interpretation would allow.

This also raises a question Viola and Barna might find uncomfortable. The domus ecclesiae was originally necessitated by persecution. As this abated, they continued meeting in house structures but now they no longer hid their activities and the structures were obviously quite impressive. One wonders if the use of the house structure had become the very sort of "tradition" Viola and Barna normally like to condemn.

The authors follow this rather clumsy attempt with another. While admitting the churches were modeled after the basilicas used for Roman governmental buildings, they claim these were patterned after earlier Greek pagan temples.[40] This reeks of an obvious attempt at throwing anything up and seeing what sticks. Even if aspects of the design were derived from earlier Greek temples, it would be irrelevant since the selection was obviously guided by the necessity of following a known pattern that could accommodate large indoor crowds and not a desire to imitate pagan worship structures. It also is an attempt to avoid the obvious fact the design was not associated with pagan temples at the time but only some aspects of its design were also used in earlier pagan temples.

This is an example of a tactic that appears throughout their book. If

---
40 *Pagan Christianity?*, 22.

Chapter 2 – Church Buildings

something was ever used by pagans prior to Christian use, then it is pagan. It does not matter if the Jews used it as well or if it was used for practical reasons and not a desire to follow pagan norms. It now has "pagan" stamped on it and can never be touched. Of course, this only applies to things the authors wish to condemn. After all, pagans had houses as well and fledgling pagan cults would also meet in homes. Don't expect consistency with this bunch.

What Viola and Barna fail to grasp is the design of these churches was as much a civil engineering issue as a religious one. It would be the Roman architects and engineers overseeing the construction and they needed to use a model that could accommodate large crowds on the scale the emperor envisioned. More importantly, there was pressure to complete it quickly and without problems so it made sense to build a structure with which they were already familiar. Given the requirements, the basilica was very much the best choice available.

Yet the attack on the basilicas is not over and it reaches a new low with a ridiculous pieces of armchair psychology. In this case, Viola and Barna assert Constantine chose the basilica model because they were wonderful for seating passive and docile crowds to watch a performance.[41] First of all, given their obvious "any stick will do" approach to criticizing Constantine, I hardly trust their insight into his motives. But worse yet, the source they cite for this outrageous claim, Michael Gough[42], says nothing of the sort.

On the page cited by Viola and Barna, Gough does indeed raise the question of whether Constantine specifically chose the basilica model but he never attributes the motives assigned by the authors. This is an important point since the emperor having a role in the process is not disputed – after all, he was financing the construction. The allegation Viola and Barna make in this statement is that one of his reasons was to create a passive audience – a point never even discussed in the source.

---

41 *Pagan Christianity?*, 22.
42 *Pagan Christianity?*, 22n85.

24   The New Restorationists

Moreover, Gough gives an entirely different reason for the selection:

> Those who suggest that the choice of the basilica was due to a direct initiative of Constantine, and that he was influenced in that choice by the audience halls incorporated in the imperial palaces, very rightly stress in support of their theory the suddenness and speed with which this basically simple plan was adopted, and then spread during the fourth century throughout the Roman Empire. Indeed, so far as the choice of a specialized building is concerned, the imperial example in Rome, Constantinople, Jerusalem and Bethlehem may well have played a decisive role; but in the present writer's view, it is far more likely that the basilical plan imposed itself on Constantine's architects than that it was consciously imposed by the Emperor on his Christian subjects. It is, in fact, quite reasonable to ask what type of building then in common use, other than the basilica, would have been so suitable or so readily adaptable to the needs of congregations attending the celebration of the Eucharist.[43]

Thus, Gough actually concluded the choice was a practical one forced by the triple dictates of the nature of Christian worship, the emperor's desire for a grand structure, and the engineers' need for a familiar pattern that meets both of the other requirements. Viola and Barna's accusations are nothing more than innuendo based upon their own presuppositions and is contradicted by their own source!

   Anyone familiar with the controversies of the post-Constantinian period would know the crowds in these basilicas were anything but docile and theological controversies often ended in riots. The authors are anachronistically projecting the passivity of later developments in the West back upon the church of the early councils. The later Catholic

---

43   Michael Gough, *The Early Christians* (Frederick A. Praeger, 1961).

Chapter 2 – Church Buildings 25

passivity in worship among the laity had far more to do with the feudal system inherited from the conquering Franks than anything inherent in basilicas.

Even worse, Viola and Barna's very assertion contains an obvious faux pas. Their assertion about it seating docile crowds ignores the fact that the congregants were not seated! Even more staggering, this is something the authors acknowledge just twelve pages later![44] But they are criticizing pews at that point and now they are criticizing Constantine and so the facts may change to fit their accusations.

This playing loose with the truth is evident again in Viola and Barna's citing of Dom Gregory Dix in their description of the sanctuary[45] and attributing Dix's points about the seating of the bishops, elders, and deacons[46] to the basilica.[47] However, when one checks Dix, the description is from a chapter on the primitive liturgy of the earlier period. That is, Dix is describing the setup of the domus ecclesiae – not the basilicas. This should have been apparent by Dix's noting the setup was likely in place by the end of the first century.

The accusations just pile one on top of the other in an obvious attempt to overwhelm the reader when in reality a heavy percentage are misrepresentations or complete fabrications. It is not far from the sort of accusations made against Christianity in general through efforts such as *Zeitgeist* and *The God Who Wasn't There*. All seek to tear down the existing Church with the difference that Viola and Barna seek to replace it with their idealized version of how it should operate.

Even innocuous items come into question. The basilicas were built so the sunlight would fall upon the speaker as he faced the congregation. Rather than make the obvious deduction that this was an ingenious way of lighting the interior and making the speaker visible in the days before

---

44 *Pagan Christianity?*, 34.
45 *Pagan Christianity?*, 23.
46 *Pagan Christianity?*, 23 n98.
47 *Pagan Christianity?*, 24.

26 *The New Restorationists*

electricity, Viola and Barna cite it as evidence that Constantine was a sun worshipper![48]

At points the criticism takes on a humorous note as when they criticize Constantine for not destroying pagan temples at the beginning of a paragraph and then by the end of the paragraph they criticize him because materials stripped from destroyed pagan temples were used to build new churches on what had been pagan temple sites.[49] So he is wrong for both destroying and not destroying pagan temples. It is quite obvious the authors are less concerned with the state of pagan temples than they are in whining about Constantine.

One further piece of evidence in their sloppy handling of sources can be seen when their use of Will Durant. Pointing to their claims of the "paganization" of Christianity, they use Durant's comment that "pagan isles remained in the spreading Christian see" in reference to this process. But is that what Durant had in mind when he wrote it? Checking the source in context, we have:

> Constantine had discouraged, but not forbidden, pagan sacrifices and ceremonies; Constans forbade them on pain of death; Constantius ordered all pagan temples in the Empire closed, and all pagan rituals to cease. Those who disobeyed were to forfeit their property and their lives; and these penalties were extended to provincial governors neglecting to enforce the decree. Nevertheless, pagan isles remained in the spreading Christian sea.[50]

Thus, in context, the subject is the decline of paganism and the pagan worship continuing in pockets as the world grew Christian around them. It has nothing at all to do with a blending of Christianity and paganism.

None of this is to let Constantine off the hook for his questionable acts.

---
[48] *Pagan Christianity?*, 22.
[49] *Pagan Christianity?*, 24.
[50] Will Durant, *The Age of Faith* (Simon and Schuster, 1950), 8.

Chapter 2 – Church Buildings

Like many influential rulers of antiquity, he was very much a mixed bag. But it is quite obvious that Viola and Barna have no interest in being fair in their assessment of either him or the process leading to the construction of the basilicas. All of this and subsequent eras of the Church must be vilified to make sense of their own reconstruction program and so they rewrite history to suit their goals. At this point, we must simply step back and call them on their distortions.

Where, may I ask, is their detailed discussion of the Councils of Nicea, Constantinople, Ephesus, and Chalcedon. Were these not important accomplishments that defended the faith against heresy? Do they acknowledge the correctness of the Nicene Creed or do they think parts should be repealed? Which of the sources they cite actually agree with their assessment of church buildings? Why are they citing sources describing the domus ecclesiae and blaming it on Constantine? It is very obvious their use of sources in this matter is highly questionable and until they can answer such questions, there is no reason to take their judgments on these matters seriously.

2.5 – Gothic Cathedrals

The reign of Constantine does not end the animosity towards church buildings as Viola and Barna next take aim at just about every architectural configuration throughout history. The aim is to place any development that leads to a "church" rather than meeting in homes as some sort of compromise with paganism.

If you read Viola and Barna's version of the development of church architecture and check their claims against their sources, the same problems arise as with their earlier treatment of Constantine and the basilicas. Again, there is no attempt to fairly evaluate the evidence. This is simply a polemical attack without any pretense of rational discussion.

28   *The New Restorationists*

Take for instance their treatment of Gothic cathedrals. Noting sources that describe the use of color and light to create the effect of the New Jerusalem, they then proceed to declare the whole thing pagan.[51] At this point, one might wonder exactly what part of the New Jerusalem is pagan but that is lost in the onslaught of charges to follow.

Their argument for a pagan connection relies upon Plato stating light and color can induce moods to bring one closer to the Eternal Good. The rest of their deduction seems to be that Plato was Greek, Greece was pagan, and therefore using color and light are pagan.

Of course, Plato also thought the same of mathematics, so perhaps Viola and Barna think Christians should reject that as well. And the principles of formal logic were set down by his student Aristotle, so I suppose no Christian should be caught being logical about their beliefs. Apparently, the theology of the house church movement has no concept of the natural law.

The authors simply miss the message of these cathedrals when assert the cathedrals convey that "God is transcendent and unreachable – so just be awed by his majesty."[52]   The whole point of the cathedrals in the context of their theology is the earth is joined to the otherwise transcendent heaven on the altar. Strangely enough, they say as much by citing Harold W. Turner for the point that the Gothic cathedral was the "ultimate symbol of heaven joining the earth."[53] One suspects their own theology prevented them from understanding the implications of that claim.

Perhaps the low point of their case against the cathedrals is when they follow the lead of every crackpot fundamentalist of the last century in declaring the spires of Gothic cathedrals (and the steeples of later churches) were derived from Egyptian obelisks.[54] Their evidence for this:

---

51 *Pagan Christianity?, 28-29.*
52 *Pagan Christianity?*, 30.
53 *Pagan Christianity?*, 29.
54 *Pagan Christianity?*, 31.

Chapter 2 – Church Buildings 29

both have pointed tops. Yes, it really has descended to that level.

They do try to offer a citation to back them up on this rather odd claim. They cite Edward Norman for their argument that the popes adopted the Egyptian obelisks in Rome as a symbol towards the end of the Byzantine period and this set off a process that reached its pinnacle in the Gothic cathedrals. One problem: Norman did not say any such thing.

What Norman pointed out was the towers of the cathedrals pointing to heaven had the same appeal as when the popes adopted the obelisks in Rome. He did not say they were connected at all in sequence and certainly did not state the popes did this prior to the cathedrals being constructed. His exact statement on the matter was the following:

> Like the obelisks in ancient Egypt - which were adopted by the popes of Rome for that very reason, and dispersed by them throughout Rome - the towers were monumental structures that pointed to the heavens.[55]

There is no inference of any connection or time line in that statement. All he alleged is the motivations were the same. In fact, the use of the obelisk in Rome occurred during the Renaissance – many centuries after the Gothic cathedrals!

The unfairness of their approach can be seen further in their noting Egyptian pagan structures were vertical and heavenly in their focus while Greek structures were horizontal and earthly. This point is not really disputed but at every opportunity they use this to attach vertically focused church buildings as pagan because of the Egyptians and horizontally focused church buildings as pagan because of the Greeks. Well, if both horizontally or vertically focused church buildings are pagan, do they suggest we worship in the woods – but then the pagans did that first too!

First of all, let us point out the fallacy they employ. If someone uses an architectural technique once employed by a pagan culture, they seem to believe this taints any resulting structure as pagan. This is completely

---

55 Edward Norman, *The House of God* (Thames and Hudson, 1990), 160.

30   *The New Restorationists*

ridiculous. Vertically or horizontally aligned structures are no more inherently pagan than fire or the wheel - also used by pagans before Christians. Moreover, the basic structure of homes were also designed by pagans first - does this make house churches pagan, too?

It is quite clear the objection is not to vertically or horizontally aligned church buildings but just to church buildings in general. The alignment issue is merely a smokescreen to justify their own prior judgments and has no real relevance. After all, as mentioned earlier, pagans owned houses and worshipped in houses. Why is that not an issue?

2.6 – Protestant Church Buildings

Viola and Barna then turn to Protestant church buildings and their approach is every bit as absurd there as elsewhere. They begin by claiming the reason the Reformers did not change the overall model of church buildings because they were too conditioned by Catholic thought. It never occurs to them that the reason might be because the authors' presuppositions are part of an egalitarian mindset that is rooted in postmodern America and had no place in Reformation era Europe and certainly not in late antiquity.

Architectural staples of Protestant buildings such as the the steeple are naturally pictured as pagan. The charge is basically the same as with the spires of the cathedral: it is all from pagan Egypt. It is also as ridiculous as with the cathedrals.

When Viola and Barna turn to the pulpit, they again show they cannot let the evidence speak for itself. After stating the pulpit derived from the ambo, a raised desk, in earlier churches they grudgingly admit it was adopted from the Jewish synagogues. But they cannot let this stand and add the ambo had earlier roots in the reading desks and platforms of Greco-Roman antiquity.

They provide no source for the last claim but let us assume it is true –

so what? Do desks become pagan because pagans used desks? In that case, were the scrolls used for the Biblical texts in antiquity pagan because the Egyptians were the first to use papyrus? Were our Bibles pagan because the Romans were the first to use codices in book form? Should we stop using automobiles because pagans invented the wheel?

They go on to complain about pews and some other issues but it is more of the same. By this point there is no point and they are just firing shots to make way for their new vision. Of course, all of this would depend on them having given a fair account of the previous evidence and they have fallen far short of the mark.

2.7 – Conclusion

One can certainly criticize architectural styles of buildings and there are legitimate questions that could be raised concerning their elaborateness or the cost of overhead. But all of this is lost in a barrage of accusations that are inaccurate and unfair. It is quite clear by the end of this section that Frank Viola and George Barna have no interest in presenting issues fairly. They may have some good points in criticizing church buildings but these are lost in a barrage of wild accusations that are not worthy of serious consideration.

32 The New Restorationists

Chapter 3 – Church and Liturgy

Architecture is not the only issue Frank Viola and George Barna have with how the Church has operated for the last two millennia. They are also not terribly fond of how it worships. It is not that they disagree with the order of worship but that they disagree there should be an order of worship.

3.1 – Origins of the Liturgy

Viola and Barna begin their discussion of the origin of the Protestant worship service by noting its roots are in the Gregorian liturgy of medieval Catholicism. This certainly is no surprise – the Reformers began by taking the existing service and removing what they believed to be elements added over the centuries that did not conform to Scripture. But then they go further – they seemingly pin the entire idea of the order of worship on Gregory the Great.

Even a cursory survey of the worship of the Church in the earliest centuries would dismiss this idea. The *Didache* of the late first or early second century give basic outlines for the Eucharist and baptism. Justin Martyr outlines the typical Christian service of the second century and it sounds very much like the traditional liturgy as does that of Hippolytus' description in the third. The liturgies of the Eastern Churches were also earlier and had the same basic outline. As far back as one can detect, there is a liturgy with the general order of prayers, readings, preaching, and communion. Gregory's service was itself a blend of already existing Western liturgical influences.

34   The New Restorationists

Yet none of this is ever discussed. Instead, the authors imagine the worship of the early Christians was more...well...American. They seemingly believe the early Church just sort of went with some vague notion of where the Spirit was spontaneously leading them at the moment. But is that what the New Testament describes? What we actually find are those devoted to the teaching of the Apostles[56] and not a general sharing of ideas. When controversies arose, it was the Apostles and elders who ruled[57] rather than taking a poll.

Oddly, at this point when the discussion turns to liturgy, the authors largely put aside the opinions of liturgical scholars such as Senn, White, and Dix cited earlier and focus on the views of Will Durant[58] – a popular level historical writer with no expertise in the subject. He did, however meet one of the authors' requirements: He was not a fan of anything associated with traditional Christianity.

Viola and Barna then go through a description of the changes that have occurred in Protestant worship over the centuries. From the Reformers to the modern Evangelicals, they list the changes made in worship but decide none are really enough. Luther, Calvin, and the Reformers are criticized because they did not just scuttle the whole thing and start over.

In the eyes of Viola and Barna, everything from the Gregorian Mass to the worship of the Reformers to the revivals of the Evangelicals to the singalongs of your local megachurch are pretty much the same. They cannot have any of it because it does not conform to their image of what the church should be. Like many restorationists, they seek to recreate the church from scratch but can neither give Biblical or historical arguments for their model nor explain why God allowed this situation to stand for almost the entire history of Christianity until they came along.

---

56 *Acts* 2:42.
57 See, for example, where the dispute over the Gentile mission was taken to the Apostles and elders in *Acts* 15.
58 See, for example, *Pagan Christianity?*, 51-52, where Durant is cited as the chief source on a topic with which he has little known expertise.

Chapter 3 – Church and Liturgy 35

Unlike the section on church buildings, there is little in the way of "shock value" claims. They are largely reliant upon their previous painting of the post-Constantinian church as inherently pagan and assume any connection to that church, such as that through the Gregorian liturgy, will be enough to demonstrate their point. However, since their previous assertions have already been shown to have little value, their arguments here are essentially neutralized.

The most fascinating part of the discussion is when Viola describes a "meeting" he attended of the type he has in mind.[59] It may have been a wonderful experience and I have no objections to such gatherings, but I wonder where he finds this setup in the Bible. It just is not there. But preaching, teaching, reading the Scriptures, and communion are there. So who is being Biblical and who is not?

3.2 – Sermons

Frank Viola and George Barna consider the sermon to be Protestantism's sacred cow. Here they do go into another historical analysis and it proves to be every bit as loose with the evidence as their earlier pronouncements on architecture. Again the same convoluted arguments apply: if a pagan ever did X, then X is inherently pagan. The logical fallacies of this sort of reasoning should by now be apparent.

They begin by discussing the sophists. The sophists used rhetoric and speeches and therefore they suppose any who use rhetoric and speeches are at some level sophists.[60] Apparently the authors are unaware of the fact that all A are B does not imply all B are A. Of course, this is a rule of formal logic as constructed by Aristotle and they criticize him as well.[61] At this point one wonders if they think all Christians should be illogical and inarticulate.

---

59 *Pagan Christianity?*, 78-79.
60 *Pagan Christianity?*, 89-93.
61 *Pagan Christianity?*, 90.

36   The New Restorationists

This does not mean that rhetoric and logic cannot be abused and there are obvious cases where someone has used verbal skill and hidden assumptions to "reason" their way to falsehood. But the proper use of logic to reason and the ability to convey that message to others is not something the Church should shun and it never has done so. As with other gifts, the issue is not the gift itself but how it is employed. One may use the power of reasoning and speaking for the glory of God or to deceive. It is the application and not the gift itself that separates light from darkness.

Their interpretation of how the sermon entered the church is every bit as absurd as everything else in this book. They claim a vacuum was created around the third century when mutual ministry faded from the body of Christ and the traveling Christians who spoke out of prophetic burden died out. Rather than citing someone with current expertise in church history, they rely on someone sympathetic to their movement and a lecture given in 1888.[62] Their theory then has the clergy emerging, open meetings dying out, and the development of the "service."

All of the above is without any historical evidence for it and much against it. There is no record of anything resembling the "open meetings" they claim. Every source we have describing Christian worship from the end of the Apostolic age onward points to something with the outline of the standard liturgy. As for the clergy, they were already in existence long before then. Clement of Rome defends the authority of the leadership in Corinth at the end of the first century. Around 115 A.D., Ignatius of Antioch upholds the importance of the role of bishop in the Church. There is simply no basis for their claims.

Even during the New Testament era, it was the Apostles who were doing the teaching and not having sharing sessions. How do they explain Paul speaking for hours and even renting a "pagan" lecture hall for two years? Obviously, the Apostles did not share Viola and Barna's disdain for authority, preaching, and lecturing. What Viola and Barna consider a "polluted stream" was very much part of the New Testament Church.

---

62 *Pagan Christianity?*, 91n28,29.

Chapter 3 – Church and Liturgy

They then turn to focusing on their two premier villains: Augustine and John Chrysostom. While enduring this pair whining about two of Christianity's most important figures is a test of endurance, it does provide more evidence of their amateur handling of source material. They state Chrysostom emphasized "the preacher must toil long on his sermons in order to gain the power of elegance" and reference an article by George H. Williams in a collection of essays edited by H. Richard Niebuhr and Daniel D. Williams.[63] However, when one checks the source, the statement is not by Chrysostom at all but a comment by the author leading up to a description of the relationship between then presbyter Chrysostom and his bishop at Antioch.[64]

The problem again is they believe something used by someone pagan is then inherently pagan even if it had nothing to do with the celebration of pagan religions. Christians have no reason to disregard what are essentially secular developments just because they were originally done by pagans. By this reasoning, then logic (Aristotle), mathematics (Euclid), medicine (Galen), and history (Herodotus) are inherently pagan as well and we should have nothing to do with them.

3.3 – Conclusion

Viola and Barna move on to various approaches in the Protestant world and I do not seek to defend everything they attack. There indeed is a lot wrong with the Church today but it has nothing to do where they place the blame. The whole problem with much of the Church is they have no idea of their purpose: to bring us in direct contact with God's Word so we may be aware both of our own guilt and of God's grace through Jesus Christ. Unfortunately, it has often turned into pop psychology sessions dispensing practical advise about raising children or having a better marriage or

---

63 *Pagan Christianity?*, 94.
64 The article may be viewed online at <http://www.religion-online.org/showchapter.asp?title=408&C=165> (Accessed May 5, 2010).

entertainment that has little to do with the faith except at a very superficial level.

We live in a culture that promotes egalitarian ideals and eschews any sense of tradition, authority, and structure. So when someone comes along and asserts we should do away with tradition, authority, and structure, it is legitimate to ask whether they are advocating Biblical or cultural norms.

Chapter 4 – Church Authority

If there is one thing Frank Viola and George Barna are sure about, it is that the Church has no biblical basis for hierarchy. Their opposition to the Church buildings and the liturgy actually grow out of this dislike of such offices among Christians. They are sure it has no Biblical basis and should be tossed aside. But how well does their beliefs stand up to the facts?

4.1 – Hierarchy in the New Testament

Before dealing with Viola and Barna's claims, let us see what the New Testament has to say about authority in the Church. One of the first things the Apostles do after Jesus' ascension is decide to choose a successor to Judas among the Apostles[65] – an odd thing to do if their were no offices. They even quote Psalm 109:8 for "Let another man take his office."[66] Asking for guidance from the Lord, they pray for Him to indicate which one of these men should "take the place in this ministry and apostleship from which Judas turned aside to go to his own place"[67] – again an odd thing to do were there no office at stake.

After Pentecost, did the early Church devote itself to sharing and learning about the Lord together? No, they devoted themselves to the

---

65 *Acts* 1:15-26.
66 *Acts* 1:20.
67 *Acts* 1:25.

40   The New Restorationists

Apostles' teaching, fellowship, the breaking of bread, and the prayers.[68] The prayers refers to the prayers of the Jews at the appointed hours[69] while the breaking of bread indicates the feast the Lord had ordained and was alluded to when he met the disciples on the road to Emmaus and revealed Himself "in the breaking of bread."[70]

Nor were the signs and wonders an egalitarian event but they were given "through the apostles."[71] In fact, the responsibility of public witnessing was commissioned to the Apostles and the direction of this witnessing was their responsibility.[72] Further evidence of their authority is shown by those entering the Church laying their wealth from selling worldly goods not at the congregations' feet but at the Apostles' feet.[73] We even see the judgment of God declared by Peter upon those who withheld the full share![74]

When a dispute over the distribution of food to the widows arose, it was not decided by the group as a whole but brought to the Apostles. They had the disciples choose seven men among them for this task and stated they would then appoint them.[75] Clearly, the selection by the people was not enough – the choice had to be ratified by entrusted with authority in the Church. The Apostles then granted them the authority for this task by the laying on of hands.[76]

When Philip witnessed in Samaria, he healed and converted many and baptized them[77], but it was necessary for two of the Apostles to go there so the new converts might fully receive the Holy Spirit.[78] Why would this be

---

68 *Acts* 2:42.
69 *Acts* 3.1.
70 *Luke* 24:13-35.
71 *Acts* 2:43; also see *Acts* 5:12.
72 *Matthew* 28:16-20; *Acts* 1:22.
73 *Acts* 4:35.
74 *Acts* 5:1-11.
75 *Acts* 6:3.
76 *Acts* 6:5.
77 *Acts* 8:12.
78 *Acts* 8:14-15.

Chapter 4 – Church Authority   41

if there were no distinctions in the ranks of believers?

The greatest internal dispute in the first few decades of the Church was the controversy over the mission to the Gentiles. Peter, when he has his vision, is instructed various animals that would be considered unclean and his reply is "By no means, Lord; for I have never eaten anything that is common or unclean."[79] Thus we see at this point Peter was still observing Jewish dietary restrictions. Later when he meets Cornelius, he makes quite clear that, until that point, the Christians had separated themselves from the gentiles.[80]

The matter finally came to a head at what is often called the Council of Jerusalem. The Church decided to meet over the matter of the mission to the Gentiles and whether they needed to eventually observe the Mosaic Law. What is interesting is this matter is not brought up before the whole congregation but only the Apostles and elders[81] – that is, the leaders. Hence, you have a decision being rendered by the leadership and then agreed upon by the congregation as a whole[82] and then sent by letter to other churches.[83]

The case of James, the brother of the Lord also gives us insight into the emerging hierarchy. It is clear that after the main body of the Apostles left Jerusalem, he took over leadership in the church there and served the role of what would be a rabbi in Judaism or the bishop later in the church's history. We can see his special status just by noting the treatment of him in passages of the New Testament during this period.

Notice, for example, that when an angel rescues Peter, the Apostle singles James out for special mention in giving instructions that word of his rescue be told to "James and to the brothers."[84] At the Council of

---

79 *Acts* 10:14.
80 *Acts* 10:28-29.
81 *Acts* 15:6.
82 *Acts* 15:22.
83 *Acts* 15:22-23.
84 *Acts* 12:17.

42   The New Restorationists

Jerusalem, it is James who makes the final decision on the matter by giving his judgment.[85] When Paul visits Jersualem he meets James who is again singled out as more than just a mere elder.[86] Paul gives us further details by noting that he recognized early on that James along with Cephas (Peter) and John were pillars[87] and James had the status of an Apostle.[88] In the dispute with Peter over the latter's withdrawal from eating with the gentiles, he describes those from Jerusalem as having been sent by James.[89] None of this makes any sense if James is not in a position of leadership and every mention of the Church in Jerusalem after the Apostles had left shows them deferring to James' leadership.

There are numerous places where the New Testament outlines the qualifications, responsibilities, and method of selection for the overseers/elders, and deacons.[90] The emerging structure of the Church is thus set out before us in the New Testament and was well established by the second century. For anyone to assert the New Testament does not present a hierarchy in the Church is beyond misleading.

4.2 – Pastoral Offices

Despite all the evidence to the contrary, Viola and Barna insist there did not exist any official leadership and that the New Testament makes this clear. Of course, they discuss no Scripture in their assertions and they have no real historical evidence. The best evidence they can muster are at best misdirecetions.

For example, they claim the elders of the church had no hierarchy *among themselves*. Whatever the truth of this statement – it appears it

---

85 *Acts* 15:19.
86 *Acts* 21:18.
87 *Galatians* 2:9.
88 *Galatians* 1:19.
89 *Galatians* 2:12.
90 *Acts* 14:23; *Acts* 15; *Acts* 16:4; *Acts* 20:17-32; *Acts* 21:17-18; *Philippians* 1:1; *I Timothy* 3:1-13; *I Timothy* 4:14-16; *Titus* 1:5-9.

varied from place to place – they ignore the fact that even in areas ruled by a council of elders, this group itself formed a hierarchy in that local church. Hierarchy does not imply a monarchial setup – oligarchy is a hierarchy as well.

They point to Ignatius of Antioch as a turning point as though he single handedly created the office of bishop. However, he actually knew the Apostles and was placed into his position during the Apostolic period and likely by one of them. Nor was his position, as contended, unique in the Church: Polycarp held the bishopric at Smyrna, Papias at Hieropolis, and presumably others did at the cities to whom Ignatius writes emphasizing the bishops' importance. There were also some areas that did not have the episcopate. The case of Clement of Rome is disputed because it is not clear exactly what position he held. Regardless, all of these have some degree of precedent in the case of James mentioned earlier.

One point needs to be made about Ignatius and other Church Fathers in connection to the episcopate of this era. There is a tendency for those on both sides of the question to anachronistically read back later developments into this earlier period. Thus, when one sees the word "bishop," an immediate connection is made to some guy in fancy robes getting his ring kissed. This concept would have been completely alien to the early bishops.

The Greek word "episkopos," often translated "bishop," actually means "overseer" and this was the role intended: to oversee the Church. When Ignatius writes of the importance of following the bishop, he is referring to the particular context of the early second century when the Church was faced with various Gnostic groups preaching another Jesus. Ignatius pointed to the bishops set in place by the Apostles as the sign of continuity with their teachings and was never intending to project any sort of "blind acceptance" into future centuries. It should also be pointed out that Ignatius saw the role of the bishop as clearly inferior to that of the Apostles.[91] If one translates his title as "overseer" or even "pastor,"

---

91 Ignatius wrote in his Epistle to the Romans that he does not issue commands to them

44   The New Restorationists

opinions on Ignatius might change drastically.

These sorts of misconceptions plague Viola and Barna's work throughout their discussion. Because the roles of the pastoral offices were clearly not offices wielding temporal power as in the medieval period, they just assume they did not exist. The authors are simply unable to read the patristic witness on its own terms and time and time again project their own preconceived ideas upon the period without evidence – even when these claims contradict those claims of both the New Testament and the early patristic authors.

Nowhere is this more clearly seen than is their discussion of ordination. Despite all the evidence the Apostles directed the selection of positions in the Church with qualifications made and the laying on of hands to raise them to this status, Viola and Barna insist it was all just an informal process that just occurred informally without any need for permanent offices. This is simply ridiculous as any reading of the New Testament passages indicated in the prior section make evident. Moreover, it is nothing more than the reading back into the first century of postmodern American values with no place there.

There can be legitimate disputes over exactly what sort of ministry the Apostles had in mind. However, there is no disputing there was a ministry and the Apostles were above all others in that ministry. The metaphor used for the Church is the body of Christ and, like any body, each part has its function. But some parts do in fact govern others and the head governs all. A body is not an amorphous blob with different parts taking on different roles at different times but a well defined organism with all having a role and some of those roles involve directing other parts under the direction of the head of the body.

---

as did Peter and Paul as they were Apostles.

4.3 – Conclusion

It is astounding that Viola and Barna believe they know the New Testament Church better than those who actually knew the Apostles – men like Clement, Polycarp, and Ignatius. As the Church endured persecution and these men were willing to pay the ultimate price, all our postmodern authors can see is corruption and compromise. At every era, they find fault in martyrs for no other reason than they bear witness that the early Christians did not have the mindset of postmodern Americans.

None of this is to claim the early Church – or any period of the Church's history – is beyond criticism. The problem is that the authors are so blatantly one-sided in their presentation that any legitimate point becomes lost amidst historical nonsense and bad citations.

Chapter 5 – Sacraments of the Church

Viola and Barna naturally decide the Sacraments of the Church are in need of overhaul as well. I will not address the issues of when baptism should be administered and to whom or the exact nature of what happens at communion – these questions have been points of controversy for centuries and they will certainly not be settled in a side comment here. Instead, I will focus on inaccuracies in their treatment that are matters of the New Testament and patristic accounts.

5.1 – Baptism

Viola and Barna concentrate on only two aspects of baptism – the delay in baptism from the second and third centuries and the sinner's prayer. In the first case, the situation facing the early Church – persecutions, heresies, and other elements that might lead them to enure the candidate was serious and understood the Christian message is never really addressed. As with everything else, the worse possible motives are simply assumed and hence their treatment is not worthy of serious consideration.

As for the sinner's prayer, it was an outgrowth of modern American Evangelicalism. They treat it as though this were the replacement for baptism among many Christians when in reality it is primarily within the American Evangelical movement. While I would agree it is a recent addition to and distortion of the faith, I would point out it is no more so than many of their own suggestions. Both are rooted in projecting American sensibilities onto the faith of the Apostles.

5.2 – Lord's Supper

Nowhere are the authors' contemporary American sensibilities more on display than on their treatment of the Lord's Supper. Viola and Barna argue it was no more than a festive meal shared in someone's living room. Of course they merely assert this – no Scripture is quoted and no early Church source is cited. It is no more than their own presuppositions.

The first error they make is to assume a shared meal and a liturgical act are cannot be connected. That is, they assume the Lord's Supper could not have been a ritual or liturgical act because it was a shared meal. This demonstrates a complete ignorance of the practices of Judaism then and now since the context of the Last Supper was a ritual meal known as the Passover.

On Passover was the Jews consumed the sacrifice of the paschal lamb in remembrance of God freeing them from bondage in Egypt. The early Christians would understand the bread and wine though Christ's own words as His body and blood, the body and blood of the Lamb of God, and they gathered to remember Him who freed them from the bondage of death.

The most thorough description of the Lord's Supper appears in I Corinthians which was written prior to the Gospels and their accounts of the Last Supper. Paul does not need to reveal the existence of the ritual to the Church in Corinth, but only chide them for their irreverence in its celebration. His exposition, though occasioned by their misdeeds, provides far more information than many suspect.

First of all, Paul writes of the divisions in Corinth and states it is not he Lord' Supper they eat when they gather together.[92] He then condemns their actions and implies their main focus should not be eating and drinking for he openly reminds them they have their own houses where

---

92 I Corinthians 11:17-20.

Chapter 5 – Sacraments of the Church

they can eat and drink.[93] He then states their real purpose is to commemorate the Lord's act of redemption through the words and actions he performed as part of the ritual meal on the night he was betrayed.[94] Even the words of institution emphasizes the real purpose is not to have a potluck dinner but to do this in remembrance of Him.

The seriousness of the undertaking is seen further by Paul declaring the nature of this feast. It is not some mere gathering of Christians for a meal but a proclamation of the Lord's death until He comes again.[95] He declares those that eat and drink in an unworthy manner profane the body and blood of Christ.[96] He calls for self-examination and discernment[97] before participation so judgment may not come upon them[98] as it already had upon others.[99] This is not a mere meal but a participation in the body and blood of Christ that through it the many are one body.[100]

It should also be noted that in all the descriptions of the feast in the Gospels, the Epistles of Paul, and other passages that may be allusions to them, only the bread and cup are mentioned. It is assumed and certainly rightly so that other things were part of the meal but they obviously were not essential. Nor do we find anything mentioned in the writings of the Church for the centuries that follow other than the bread and cup. Details are given in the Didache and Justin Martyr and elsewhere but there is no mention of anything not related to the bread and cup. They simply were not necessary.

All of this is as background to Viola and Barna's treatment of the separation of the sharing of the bread and cup from a more general meal. They make assumptions withou t reference to the primary sources. In fact,

---

93 I Corinthians 11:21-22.
94 I Corinthians 11:23-25.
95 I Corinthians 11:26.
96 I Corinthians 11:27.
97 I Corinthians 11:28, 31.
98 I Corinthians 11:29
99 I Corinthians 11:30.
100 I Corinthians 10:16-17.

50 The New Restorationists

their timeline is quite ridiculous. They claim the separation of the bread and cup from a meal did not begin until the time of Tertullian. Now given Tertullian was born around 160 A.D., one would expect this to begin no earlier than approximately 185 A.D. with completion about 200 A.D.

So let us check the worship decades prior to Tertullian as described by Justin Martyr at about 150 -160 A.D. In the *First Apology*, he writes:

> And on the day called Sunday, all who live in cities or in the country gather together to one place, and the memoirs of the apostles or the writings of the prophets are read, as long as time permits; then, when the reader has ceased, the president verbally instructs, and exhorts to the imitation of these good things. Then we all rise together and pray, and, as we before said, when our prayer is ended, bread and wine and water are brought, and the president in like manner offers prayers and thanksgivings, according to his ability, and the people assent, saying Amen; and there is a distribution to each, and a participation of that over which thanks have been given, and to those who are absent a portion is sent by the deacons.[101]

Thus the separation Viola and Barna assumed first appeared in the late second century was apparently well established decades earlier.

Moreover, the Didache instructs the Church to "break bread" each Sunday, describes it as the sacrifice predicted in Malachi, and gives liturgical instructions on the prayers over the bread and wine.[102] So we now see this practice may well go back to the end of the Apostolic age if not earlier. Nor are they correct in placing the term "Eucharist" at that late period. It is used by the *Didache*, Ignatius of Antioch, and Justin Martyr and the matter of fact way it is presented presumes it was a common term by then. This is not surprising given it is from the Greek of the New Testament account.

---

[101] Justin Martyr, *First Apology*, Chapter 67.
[102] *Didache*, Chapters 9-10, 14.

Thus at almost every level, Viola and Barna get it wrong. Whatever the reason for the separation of the bread and cup from the general meal, there was never any indication the other food was of any importance. Nor did any Christian of the first few centuries ever described it as a mere gathering for a dinner in someone's living room. Whatever Viola and Barna may have been describing, it was not the Lord's Supper.

5.3 – Conclusion

Viola and Barna have simply assumed their conclusions were unassailable and critiqued everything in terms of them. There was no attempt to address Holy Scripture, just the assumption it agreed with them. There certainly was no desire to familiarize themselves with the writings of the early Christians. As with other elements of their ideas, their understanding of the development of Christian doctrine was found wanting. It is all based on presuppositions and little else.

Chapter 6 – Miscellaneous Issues

There are a few other topic Viola and Barna mention that are side issues to those discussed already. A few short examples should suffice.

6.1 – Christian Education

As with everything else, Viola and Barna merely assume some vague definition of "organic community" to define how the teaching of the Church was passed on to future generations. There is no proof offered for any of this – certainly no evidence is forthcoming in the book aside from quoting other authors in the movement. Nor is any attempt made to explain how investigate how information was passed on in the context of Second Temple Judaism. In their rant against Christian education, the authors only demonstrate why it is so needed.

There are four models presented for the education of leaders: Episcopal, Scholastic, Seminarian, and the Bible College. There again is the outlook that schools were instituted earlier by Greeks, the Greeks were pagan, and therefore these schools were influenced by paganism. One wonders if the authors had availed themselves of any of the Greek wisdom they criticized, whether they would finally understand the logical fallacies inherent in such a view. They also avoid the uncomfortable fact that Paul taught the faith in a setup very much like a Greek philosophical school.[103]

Criticism is also given for the idea of the Sunday School for the Church

---

[103] *Acts* 19:9.

in general. Again there are the vague references to an organic approach with little in the way of details. One wonders exactly what they have in mind and whether anything is passed on at all besides their own iconoclastic tendencies.

Nowhere in any of this do they discuss exactly what it is they believe about Jesus Christ. Do they hold the doctrine of the Trinity or the two natures of Christ or don't they? And if so, then how would they express them and pass them on to other Christians?

This is not to say the Church is doing such a great job of this at the moment. Much of Christianity has descended into triviality in its presentation of the faith. However, Viola and Barna seem to think we have not gone far enough in that direction. Their vision of the Church succumbs even further to the desires of American culture and condemns the Church to become more and more about us and less and less about Christ.

6.2 – Using the Bible

Viola and Barna then turn to how the Bible is used in the Church. Strangely enough, they they end up complaining about "prooftexting" and ignoring the original context and purposes of the Biblical books. This is certainly something to criticize and far too much of it goes on in the Church. However, as has been demonstrated throughout, few are as guilty of this as Viola and Barna themselves.

Their method of understanding is to assume their contemporary egalitarian "house church" setup applied in the world of the first century Church and then force everything to fit into their model. A classic example comes when they exegete Paul and Barnabas appointing elders and declare what actually going on in Acts 14:3 is that they are publicly endorsing old men in each church.[104]

---

[104] *Pagan Christianity?*, 235.

Chapter 6 – Miscellaneous Issues

If this be so, one wonders then why so many translators render it "appointed" which certainly has another connotation from "publicly endorsed." The answer is Viola and Barna are just plain wrong. All they have done is performed an act of "eisegesis" whereby they see themselves in the passage. They have a conclusion and fixed the meaning of the verse to conform to their existing opinions.

The Greek word in question is χειροτονήσαντες which means to vote by stretching out one's hand or to appoint. It does not mean a mere public endorsement but involves selection. Also, the term "elder" is derived from Judaism where it was as with the early Church a role of leadership and not just an old man. It was an office and the authors are merely pouring into the language their own meanings without any historical or linguistic justification. They just made things up to fit their views.

6.3 – Conclusion

Throughout their book, the work of the Church is criticized with only vague solutions offered in their place. The Scriptures are decontextualized and first century Judeans are transformed into postmodern Americans preaching a gospel of egalitarianism that would have been as foreign to them as televised football games. They have merely employed the same strategy as those on the most liberal ends of the theological spectrum. We have had the Marxist Jesus, the feminist Jesus, the cynic Jesus, and other ad nauseum and now they give us the therapeutic Jesus. Worshipping God is now about getting together and sharing what the Lord is doing in your life this week. It is all about you and is as vacuous as it gets.

Chapter 7 – Final Conclusions

Frank Viola and George Barna have issued a challenge to the Church. That is in itself not a bad thing. The Church definitely needs to be challenged as it has often strayed from its essential goals to spread the Gospel to the world. However, change for the sake of change is not a proper solution to those problems. It must be rooted in the Word of God.

It both their analysis of the problems and their proposed solutions, the program they present is a failure. One cannot build a house on sand and yet the very program they propose is built on fantasies about church history that do not stand up to serious scrutiny. The Church was rooted in Judaism, it did have offices, it did use a liturgy, and buildings were largely irrelevant.

One can criticize the style of buildings or our current focus in leadership or the outlines of our liturgies by Biblical standards. But to say the New Testament witnesses a mandate to avoid such things is patently false. Viola and Barna wish to overturn two thousand years of the Church on their own postmodern whims. The frightening thing is how many may go along for the ride.

I challenge Viola, Barna, and those who support them to look at the evidence presented and defend their statements in light of the inconsistencies and errors I have raised. Do not merely tell me I am part of the "institutional church" and can't get it. I have raised specific issues where their exegesis is a mess and their handling of the evidence is shabby. Deal with the evidence provided and explain why any of the conclusions reached in the book could possibly stand.

58   The New Restorationists

I also challenge them to be clear about what they believe. Paul warned about those preaching a "different Jesus" and I wonder about the Jesus of Viola and Barna. What do they believe about Jesus and how will they pass this on to future generations? Is their Jesus fully God and fully man and the incarnate Second Person of the Trinity or would they change things around a bit? I will assume they hold the orthodox position of most Christians but then their criticism of the use of philosophy by Christians is hypocritical since the terms used to define those doctrines (person, substance, hypostasis, etc.) are straight out of Greek philosophy. Or do they have a different definition?

There is nothing that Viola and Barna have proposed without severe logical and historical issues. It is a house built upon sand and I wonder how its iconoclastic tendencies will play out. The history of such movements does not fill one with confidence as they often end in repeated divisions and heresies with later followers striking off into territory the founders may not have approved.

At that point, we may all be picking up the pieces...

Appendix – Book Review

The following is a book review I wrote for my website Christianbookreviews.net:

The phenomenon of restorationism (a church body asserting its intentions to recreate the New Testament Church) is not a new one to American Evangelicalism. Generally initiated by those who have little or no understanding of the culture, history, and religious practices of those they wish to emulate, the temptation of a do-it-yourself ecclesiology (with the New Testament as their alleged guide) is irresistible for those feeling alienated by existing church practices.

The telltale signature of restorationist movements is to proclaim existing ecclesial structures to be hopelessly out of step with true Christianity. After all, if the Church needs to be restored, then one would assume something had gone terribly wrong else the entire project of restoration would be a colossal waste of time. Unlike reform movements, whose primary motivation is to pressure the existing Church to renew itself from within, the strategy for restorationists is to wipe the slate clean and imagine the Church could be restarted anew. The inevitable result is the affirmation of their own personal beliefs and practices covered by the authority of eisegetic interpretations of Scriptural passages devoid of any context apart from their own.

The latest installment of this characteristically American enterprise is now enshrined in Frank Viola and George Barna's *Pagan Christianity?*. Seeking to justify their own peculiarly postmodern American manifestation of what they believe to be "New Testament Christianity", they combine their own prejudices with such a staggering display of

60   The New Restorationists

historical ignorance, that any informed reader is left shaking their heads at their garbled understanding of the Church's past. In their attacks on anything that smells of structure or authority, one can detect a sense of glee as they engage in their ill-informed attempts at iconoclasm.

Of course, the church that "emerges" from their deconstruction is remarkably like the sort of thing that would be hatched in the mind of a postmodern American with a disdain for hierarchy, tradition, and anything that might have been considered to be of enduring value prior to their own personal conversion. Their "analysis" is a mishmash of outdated secondary sources, out-of-context quotations, unsupported hypotheses, and personal prejudices amalgamated into an "any stick will do" style attack on historical Christianity. Even worse, on those occasions where legitimate experts on the field are cited (i.e., Dom Gregory Dix, Paul F. Bradshaw, Alexander Schmeman) their views are taken so out of context as to have them seemingly ally with the authors when in fact their views are quite the opposite.

Like other revisionists on both the left and right of the ecclesial spectrum, there is an overt removal of the New Testament Church from both the context of the Jewish practice that preceded it and the ecclesial practice that followed it. Once the Church is decontextualized, the inferred meanings of the texts of the New Testament are removed and new meanings assigned. In this sense, restorationists are best seen as sharing the deconstructionist methodology common to many postmodern revisionist thinkers.

Viola and Barna begin their argument with an assault on church buildings. Their concern is not any particular problem with architectural style or the lavishness of furnishings but over the very idea of buildings being used for the specialized purpose of Christian gatherings. While the reason given for this aversion to architectural utility is passages in the New Testament that state the early Christians met in each others homes, the hidden reason is likely that one of the authors has been involved for two decades in the "house church" movement and seems to have made an idol out of a situation that grew out of necessity, was not intended as representative of a command, and was not in fact even followed strictly at the time.

The fact is that the Book of Acts clearly state that the early Christians continued to worship in the Temple and the synagogues and largely carried on the established practices of Judaism. It is only where it came to the specifically Christian cultic practices among that they retreated to their homes – the only place available for them to freely express their faith in Christ – but there is no indication that it was ever intended as normative.

They go on in rapid fire succession to rattle off a series of complaints against church buildings with allegations of their history that have little or no historical support. Many things they claim were adopted from paganism were also present in the Biblical faith of the Jews that God commanded. It never occurs to the authors the same church they accuse of importing paganism is the one that was laying down its lives in martyrdom for its refusal to compromise with paganism.

Their claim that there were no special places of worship prior to Constantine also does not stand up to careful scrutiny. Yes, they often met in houses, but these "houses" were often the villas of wealthy members of the Church. It was common for expensive homes in the Roman era to have special rooms set aside for cultic purposes and these served as places of worship for the local Christian community. There were also theological schools in places like Alexandria and Antioch that developed (a point the authors acknowledge) and these likely also had places of worship associated with them. There have been numerous archaeological finds that have discovered pre-Constantinian Christian worship spaces that were obviously set apart for that purpose. The reason for having few specifically constructed church buildings was simply that Christianity was for much of the first few centuries a persecuted religion In times of severe persecution, the Christians often had to meet in total secrecy and places like the Catacombs in Rome and other secluded spots were employed. Once the persecution ended, such restrictions were abandoned. The authors make much of the grandeur of the basilicas built by Constantine, but fail to mention such notable places were pilgrimage sites and hardly the norm. In most of the Roman Empire, local churches would continue to be rather humble affairs.

The authors' biases are again on display as they go as far in their tirades as to claim Jesus had a negative view of the Temple. Forgetting that the construction of both Jewish temples were ordained by God, they completely distort the obvious meaning of the passage – a negative view of the Jewish authorities – and transfer the negative view to the Temple itself. Jesus referred to the Temple as His Father's House – it contained the very presence of God in the Holy of Holies – and, far from downplaying its significance, chased out the moneychangers for defiling it. The passages they do cite give Jesus' accusations against the Jewish leaders. His statements on the destruction of the Temple was not because the Temple was an evil but because they had rejected the very presence of God who stood before them.

The authors continually make the point that Jesus overthrew the existing Jewish structure and replaced it with a non-hierarchical, non-liturgical ekklesia. But the picture painted in the New Testament is entirely different. In Acts, it states the early Christians kept to the teachings of the Apostles, fellowship, the breaking of bread, and the prayers. In the context of the Judaism the early Christians practiced, there is definitely a hierarchy and liturgy implied in these words.

The "teaching of the Apostles" demonstrates that there were those in authority to teach the truths of the faith and authority implies hierarchy. This is bone out as the Apostles are sought out for all major decisions. When controversy erupted over Paul's mission to the Gentiles, the disagreement was brought before the Apostles and elders at Jerusalem who decided the issue in council. In his epistles, Paul makes a point that he too is an apostle and shares the same authority. Paul instructs Timothy to appoint elders in the churches; throughout the New Testament, the Apostles ordain others' ministries by the laying on of hands.

Appendix – Book Review   63

All of this should not be surprising – the early Christians did not live in an egalitarian society. Even before the Church, there is an implied hierarchy in the Gospels – Peter, James, and John form an inner circle among the twelve and every list of the twelve has Peter first and Judas last. Most importantly, there is a hierarchy within the triune God as the three persons relate to each other in hierarchical fashion. Thus, it is natural that Christ's body is also hierarchical and reflects an order.

The passages cited for their position have nothing to do with the structure of the Church. For example, they cite the worldly desires of some of the twelve who attempt political maneuvers and are rebuked – but the rebuke states nothing about the existence of hierarchy but only their worldly desires. It is quite clear that the authors have long ago came to their conclusions and now are "proof-texting" their answers with passages that have no real bearing on the subject.

The liturgical dimension of the early Christians can be seen in the phrases "the prayers" and "the breaking of bread". The prayers refer to the normal liturgical prayers of observant Jews but now given a Christian emphasis. These would develop over time into the Christian prayers of the divine office. The breaking of bread refers to the communion meal and was thought to reveal Christ to the believers (see the allusions to this in the story of the Road to Emmaus in Acts). The breaking of bread at a meal had long been a liturgical act at Jewish meals similar to our own praying grace. The Holy Communion was ordained by Christ as part of a liturgical meal celebrated by a people for whom the consumption of food followed liturgical rules. Considering that all Christian were at that point observant Jews (else the Council of Acts 15 would have been unnecessary), the thought they were somehow non-hierarchical or non-liturgical is merely an anachronistic application of postmodern American ideals on first century Near Eastern people.

Turning to the evolution of modern Protestant worship, Viola and Barna continue their pattern of misguided historical analysis. First, they infer the source of the Protestant worship was the medieval mass promulgated by

64   The New Restorationists

Gregory the Great. Here they ignore that the Gregorian Mass was an amalgamation of elements from existing Roman and Franco-Germanic liturgies and these followed the basic pattern of liturgy outlined by earlier writers such as Hippolytus and Justin Martyr and going back to the Didache at the turn of the first century. The Didache itself follows a pattern taking elements of Jewish practice that date back to the Second Temple period. This is further verified by the practices within the Byzantine Churches whose liturgy developed separately but still maintained the early structure indicated by the early Christians. Even the Church of the East, stretching from Persia to China, followed a similar pattern in its own unique liturgy despite being essentially cut off from contact with the Roman Church.

The liturgical developments within Protestantism were, not surprisingly, a mixed bag – some good (the reintroduction of preaching to a key role) and some bad (the anti-sacramental nature of much of its worship) just as the developments in the medieval West had also been much of a mixed bag. Unfortunately, many of the liturgical reforms introduced by American Protestantism is far more reflective of American culture than the practice of the early Christians. Viola and Barna's project, like other restorationist attempts, always end up telling us far more about the participants than the early Church.

Yet it is not just the most formal elements of Christian worship that the authors wish to abandon – even so basic and obvious a part of the service as the sermon is found wanting. Here the authors blame it on rhetoricians and philosophers – an assertion so absurd that it would be funny were it not the fact that the naive will take this drivel seriously. Yes, philosophers and rhetoricians often spoke at length about topics – but so did rabbis and those in authority in any endeavor. The Apostles would preach in the synagogues or in public squares where they could communicate the Good News. They also would speak at length in specifically Christian gatherings where they could teach the truths of the faith to the Church. The authors credit Augustine and Chrysostom with making pulpit oratory part of the faith – and they certainly were wonderful preachers – but fail to mention

Appendix – Book Review 65

the many great sermons (available in any collection of the ante-Nicene Church Fathers) of those who preceded them. They fail to accept that God can make use of the gifts He has bestowed that are offered to His service in love. Yes, the original twelve were largely a rather unsavory group but God had no problem making use of the obvious gifts of Paul and Luke who were clearly of a far different social strata.

As low as their opinions are of sermons, the authors think even worse of those who give them – particularly the authority attached to them. They ridiculously claim that there were no "official offices" with slots to fill, yet among the first things they did was choose a successor to replace the position of Judas in the twelve and even gave criteria for their nomination. The emergence of the office of bishop was, contrary to their claims, quite natural. As local church's reached points of self-sufficiency, they no longer needed to rely upon the evangelists or the church that had sponsored them. We see first the Church in Jerusalem having such leadership under James the Just and then both Antioch and Smyrna following under Ignatius and Polycarp. As more churches became established, the practice of episcopal leadership spread.

As mentioned earlier, the early Church had all their leadership ordained by the Apostles. We see this most clearly in Acts and in the letters of Paul. The imposition of hands was a long established practice within most cultures of the time in conferring leadership and this certainly was not lost on the early Christians. Unfortunately, this does not tickle the ears of today's trendy egalitarians and they need go to great lengths to try to make square pegs fit in round holes.

After some rather immature tirades against clerical garb and music ministries, the authors then turn their attention to the sacraments of Baptism and the Lord's Supper. Their obvious biases show by claiming the early Church practiced believers' baptism. There is in fact no evidence of this – baptism was a long standing ritual practice in Judaism (John the Baptist did not invent it) and there were no such restrictions. There are passages in the New Testament where converts' entire families were

66   The New Restorationists

baptized (presumably including small children) and Paul makes a connection between baptism and circumcision. The sacrament was the entry into the New Covenant with Christ and was open to believers and their children.

Since the early Church was growing primarily through conversion, it is natural that most early baptisms would be of adults. But you simply never hear of the children of early Christians baptized after some peculiarly American version of "being saved." They all claim to be Christians from their childhood. The only period where there was hesitation was due to some believing wrongly that there were great obstacles to salvation if they fell from the faith after being baptized and hence delayed it until close to death but this practice would be condemned.

The Lord's Supper/Communion/Eucharist was an outgrowth of Jesus' liturgical act on the night of His betrayal. The authors make much of the separation of the bread and cup from a full meal as mentioned in I Corinthians but fail to mention that Paul condemns them for their practices and replies with instructions that describe only the bread and cup. They consider the possibility that the separation was done to end abuses but then conclude it was incipient paganism. Their evidence for this: nothing. They just assume a twisted reading of the facts that concludes Christians who were willingly dying for Christ couldn't wait to be pagans. It is almost shocking to read the sheer arrogance of these two pseudohistorians who obviously not encountered the writings of the patristic Church firsthand but rely upon the inaccuracies of anti-Christian writers like Will Durant.

The reasons for later developments are quite clear if one uses the original sources and a little common sense. First of all, only the bread and cup are essential. Nothing else is mentioned in any account of the Last Supper. Then there is the implied connection with between the bread and cup and the Passover lamb. They also came to realize the connection in Hebrews as the central ritual of the priestly order of Melchizadek (a type of Christ who offered up a meal of bread and wine). The Church saw this was no mere dinner but that their sacrifice of bread and wine was being united to Christ's sacrifice on the Cross and that he was "revealed in the breaking of bread".

Of course all of this formal understanding and deep thinking about God's Holy Word is a bad idea and the authors proceed to list their complaints against every center of theological training in Church history from the great theological schools in Alexandria and Antioch to the monasteries to the medieval universities to their Protestant counterparts to the seminaries to the little Bible College down the road. Apparently, the Church would have been better off without them even though they preserved the Scriptures and kept alive the remains of Christian culture during times of great social upheaval.

Oddly enough, after giving us chapter upon chapter of some of the most horrid proof-texting ever put to print, the authors then complain about proof-texting! They also at the end introduce the idea that house churches are not always a good idea and some instruction is needed to lead them. But wait – doesn't such assistance imply something like the sort of stuff given in seminaries and doesn't the idea that some people are needed to train others institute a de facto hierarchy? Oh, and in case you are wondering where all this wonderful training is brought down to a practical level and who will be the trainers – you can get it in one of the authors' other books. One immediately is reminded of what Orwell wrote in Animal Farm: "All animals are equal, but some animals are more equal than others."

It will be interesting to see what the future holds for the house church movement. Now that so much of the patristic Church is assigned to pagan beliefs, I suspect that the formulations of faith hashed out beginning at Nicea will be called into question. One can expect to see the house churches wrestling with the same heresies the patristic Church faced as new leaders decide the early Church actually believed something else entirely. The refashioning of old heresies in new wineskins is yet another characteristic of restorationist movements.

The sort of nonsense we see in *Pagan Christianity?* is nothing new.

68   *The New Restorationists*

Hosts of restorationist movements in the past have mounted similar endeavors – each from their own uninformed perspective. While they all had their unique complaints, all had in common the elevation of American ideals to the level of divine command. For them as well as for Viola and Barna, even this error pales in comparison to their belief that their efforts are unique, revolutionary and important. How typically American!

Printed in Great Britain
by Amazon.co.uk, Ltd.,
Marston Gate.